INUIT

Helen L. Edmunds

WAYLAND

Titles in the series

Australian Aborigines
Inuit
Native Americans
Rainforest Amerindians

This title is based on Wayland's *Inuit*, in the Threatened Cultures series.

Designer: Kudos Editorial and Design Services

All photographs in this book are
© Bryan and Cherry Alexander

First published in 1995 by
Wayland (Publishers) Ltd
61 Western Rd, Hove
East Sussex BN3 1JD, England

British Library Cataloguing in Publication Data
Edmunds, Helen
   Inuit. – (Peoples Under Threat Series)
   I. Title II.
   III. Series
   305.8971

ISBN 0-7502-1419-8

Typeset by Malcolm Walker of Kudos Design
Printed and bound by Lego, Italy

Contents

1 Introduction

The Arctic sits right on top of the world, far from where the sun shines warmest. It is a frozen land: in the coldest parts the ice has not melted for tens of thousands of years.

Few creatures can live in the very heart of the Arctic, right up by the North Pole. But around its edges live seals, polar bears, whales and the Inuit people.

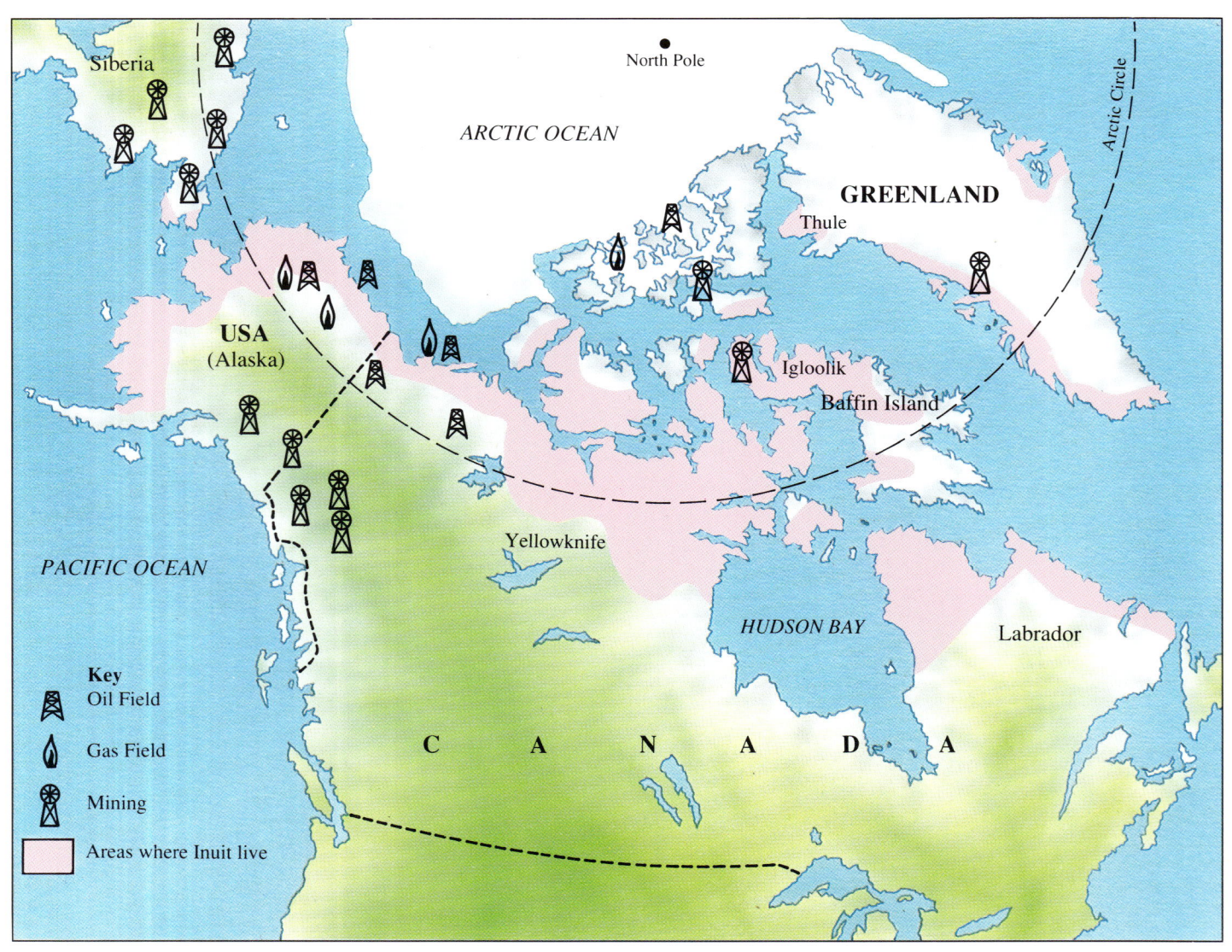

▲ *The pink areas show where the Inuit live.*

Polar night and midnight Sun

These houses in Morriussaq, an Inuit village in Greenland, were photographed at midnight. During the Arctic summer, the Earth's northern tip points at the sun. Then, the days can last for weeks, because the sun never sets. In winter the reverse is true, and the sun does not rise for weeks on end.

The Northern Lights

The Northern Lights have frightened and amazed travellers in the far north for years. They suddenly appear in the sky, constantly changing their colour and shape. Some Arctic peoples thought the Northern Lights were the dancing spirits of their ancestors.

▲ *The Northern Lights, which are sometimes called the aurora borealis. Scientists think they are caused by the Earth's magnetic field, which is very strong in the Arctic.*

For centuries, the Inuit had the Arctic to themselves. They could follow the animals they hunted all across the region. Now, other people have come to the Arctic, in search of the minerals that lie underground there. The Inuit have to share their homeland with others.

▲ *An oil rig in the heart of Alaska.*

2 Inuit Traditions

The Spirit World

In the past, all Inuit believed that all creatures – humans and animals – had a spirit. They thought that animals allowed themselves to be caught to help the Inuit survive. If things were not done correctly, the animals would not let the Inuit catch them.

▲ *The Inuit hunt walruses for their tasty meat and their ivory tusks.*

▲ *This man has hunted a polar bear. He is going to skin it.*

If Inuit hunters did not show the proper respect for the animal they hunted, their hunt was not a success. So when they cut off an animal's head, they asked its spirit to return to the wild. Sometimes, hunters would give part of the animal they killed back to the wild. Then the animal would let itself be caught again when it occupied its next body.

The Angakkug

The Inuit lived in a complicated world of spirits, which could be harmful. To help them survive, they had a person called an angakkug. The angakkug entered into a trance to find out if the spirits would allow a hunt to be successful, whether a rule had been broken, or a new baby's name.

▼ *This young girl is well wrapped up in furs to keep her warm.*

▲ *The picture above shows seal skins and meat drying in the sun. The hunters below are cutting up polar bear meat.*

Food

The Arctic is so cold that fruit and vegetables do not grow. All there is to eat is meat from the animals and fish that live there. The Inuit used to eat nothing else, but now they can buy other foods that have been flown in from outside.

▲ *An Inuit woman and her daughters shopping in Igloolik, Canada.*

Although they can buy food from shops, nearly all Inuit still go hunting. If they catch too much to eat straight away, they can store it outside in the winter. The temperature is so cold that the meat never goes bad, so the Inuit have a store of food for when the hunting is not so good.

The Inuit do not waste any part of the animals they catch. Anything edible is eaten, and they use as much of the rest of the animal as they can. Seal skins become coats, and walrus tusks make sled runners, harpoons or carvings.

Warm Clothing

In the settlements, young Inuit like to wear jeans and ski jackets. But for a hunting trip, when the weather is really cold, most Inuit prefer their old-style furs. These are warmer than anything else, because they trap heat between two thick layers of fur.

The Arctic explorer Roald Amundsen learnt how to travel across the ice sea from the Inuit. He used their techniques to reach the South Pole.

Inuit Homes

Some people think that all Inuit live in snow houses called igloos. In fact, Inuit people never lived in igloos (which they call illuviga) all the time. Igloos were just used as temporary shelters during hunting trips.

▼ *A hunter builds himself a shelter for the night.*

Traditional Inuit winter homes were half underground. They had whalebones supporting the roof, and the walls were lined with furs for warmth. In summertime, the Inuit lived in tents that were made of seal or caribou skins.

Now, most Inuit live in settlements. Their houses are flown in from further south in pieces, then put together in the Arctic.

Inuit Words

You probably already know some words of the Inuit language, without realizing it. Igloo, kayak and anorak are all Inuit words. The Inuit like to be called Inuit, not Eskimo. Eskimo is the name non-Inuit gave them, and means 'eaters of raw meat'.

This Inuit man from Greenland is using a long-handled net to catch little auks.

The Seasons

All Inuit are used to moving around as the seasons change. In winter they stay in their villages, hunting only close to home. As spring comes and the ice moves back, the hunters follow the herds of walrus as they travel north.

This hunter has shot a caribou. He is just starting to skin it. ▶

◄ *This man is using a simple hand line to fish through a hole in the ice. He already has a fine catch of Arctic char.*

During the summer, whole families leave their villages. They camp out in the wild and go hunting. The Arctic is full of creatures during the summer. Sea birds come north with the warm weather, Arctic char swim up the rivers, and whales are hunted in the fjords.

In the autumn, the weather begins to turn colder. The hunters get their dog sleds and snowmobiles ready. They know that soon the ice will be thick enough to hunt for seals as they come up at their breathing holes.

Inuit Art

The picture shows Mable Nigayath working on one of her drawings. Mable is one of several Inuit artists who have become famous. The Inuit are best known for their beautiful carvings, but some artists also make paintings.

3 Outsiders Arrive

For centuries after they first arrived in the Arctic, the Inuit had the frozen lands to themselves. Then, in the summer of 1818, the British explorer John Ross arrived at Cape York.

▼ *The grave of Alex Elder. He was a crew member on a British voyage to the Arctic in 1821-23. Like many others, he died there.*

◄ Many of the early white explorers of the Arctic were helped by the Inuit, who used dog teams just like the one in the background of this photo. Other explorers died because they refused help from the Inuit, who they thought were savages.

John Ross was followed to the Arctic by many other explorers. Some of them were searching for the North-west Passage, a short-cut to Asia from Europe. Others were trying to reach the North Pole, the northernmost point on Earth.

An American explorer, Robert Peary, was the first person to reach the North Pole. He was helped on his way by Inuit, who let him use their dogs and sleds for transport.

Minik

In 1897, Robert Peary took six Inuit from the Arctic to New York. One of them was a young boy called Minik. Minik ended up being brought up as an orphan, far from his home or family.

Arctic Whaling

At the same time as the explorers, another group of outsiders were starting to come to the Arctic seas. They were the whalers, who came to hunt the great whales. Whale oil was used for heating and light. Whalebone was used in many things, from fishing rods to women's underwear.

The whalers changed the Inuit's lives forever. They brought with them guns, knives and metal tools.

Seal Hunting

The Inuit have always hunted seals for food and clothing. Sealskins make very warm coats. Now, though, people think hunting seals is cruel. The Inuit are finding it hard to sell the skins of the seals they hunt.

◀ *This old picture shows whalers off the coast of Greenland. The whalers killed almost all the bowhead whales in the Arctic.*

Fur traders

After the whalers, fur traders began to come to the Inuit's lands. The fur trade changed the Inuit's lives in an important way. In the autumn they went out and caught animals whose furs could be exchanged for goods such as tea, coffee and tobacco. The Inuit stopped hunting just for food, and started killing more animals than they could eat. They were able to do this partly because of the modern weapons, especially guns, that they were given by the fur traders.

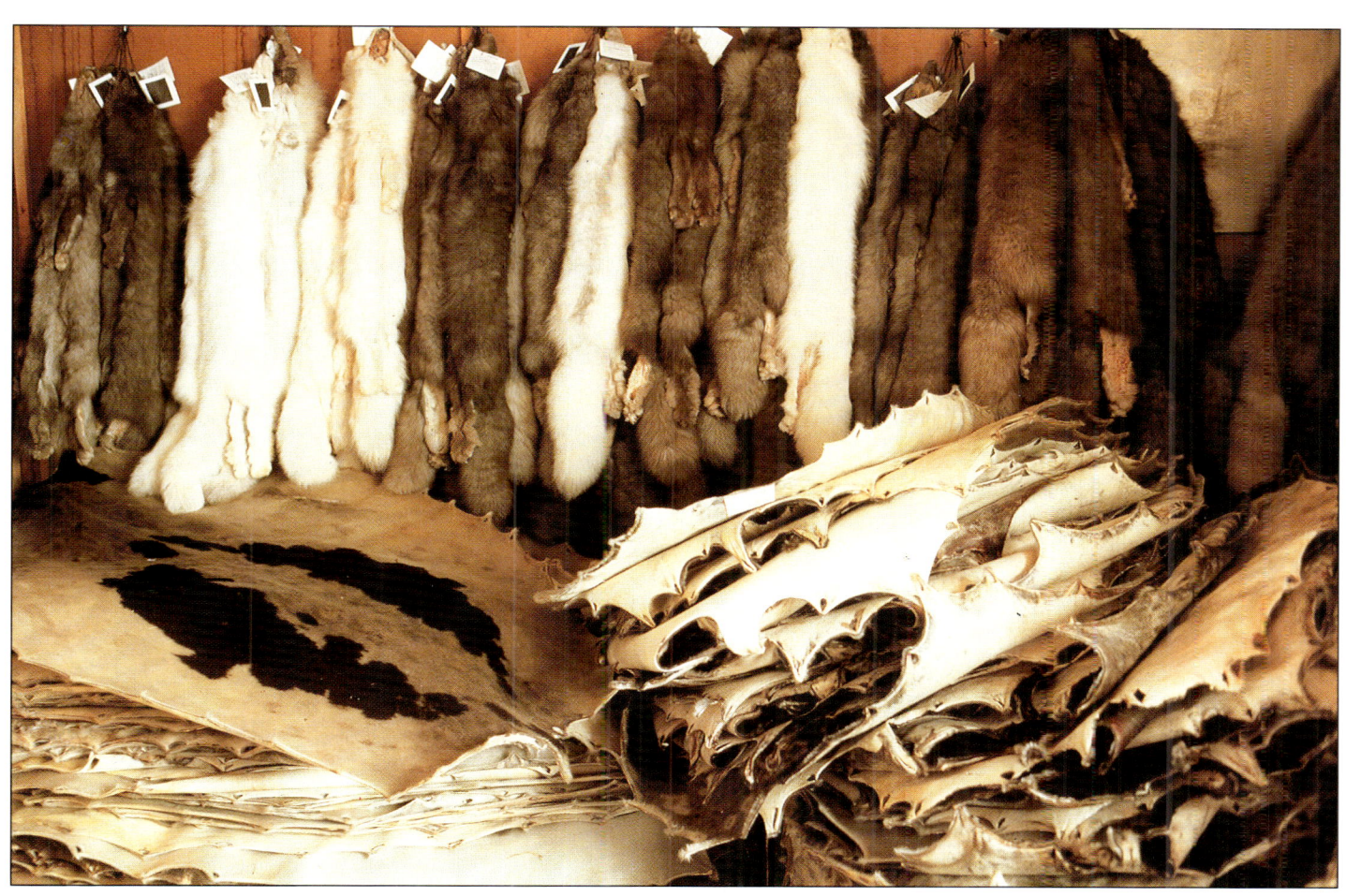

▲ *Furs ready to be sent for sale. Some people think wearing furs is cruel, and today the Inuit find it hard to sell them.*

Missionaries

Over the last 150 years, different Christian groups have sent people to live with the Inuit. They have tried to get the Inuit to abandon their old beliefs and join Christian religions. The new religions saw the world differently from the Inuit. They did not have the same respect for nature.

Many Inuit were persuaded to abandon their traditional beliefs. Now, there are Christian churches all through the arctic.

Both pictures show Christian churches in Igloolik, Canada.

▲ *Inuit children play ice hockey in the street.*

The Settlements

After the Second World War, many Inuit left their hunting lifestyle. They got jobs building defence bases in the Arctic for the government. Once the bases were built, there was no more work. But the Inuit found it hard to go back to their old lifestyle.

Other Inuit were forced to move to the new settlements when their children were taken there to go to school.

◄ *A pipeline that carries oil from the Arctic to the sea, where it is loaded on to tankers. If such pipelines leak, they damage the land.*

The government had told the Inuit that there would be jobs for them at the settlements. In fact, there were very few jobs. Most people had to depend on the government for money. The Inuit no longer had their old hunting lifestyle, but they had no work either. They were trapped.

4 Igloolik - A Canadian Village

Igloolik means 'place of houses'. It is an Inuit village deep in the Northwest Territories of Canada. The area has been hunted in by the Inuit people for at least 4,000 years. The first outsiders to visit Igloolik were led by Edward Parry in 1822.

▲ *The Inuit village of Igloolik in the Canadian Arctic.*

▲ *Shoppers load their snowmobile outside the Hudson's Bay store.*

In 1939, the Hudson's Bay Company started a trading post at Igloolik. Suddenly it was a meeting point for the whole area. Then, in 1956, the village began to grow. The government had decided to build a defence base nearby. New homes were built, and so were schools and hospitals. Many Inuit decided to move there.

◀ *The old ways mix with the new in Igloolik. People still go hunting, but they may go on snowmobiles rather than on dog sleds.*

Now, 1,000 people live in Igloolik. The village has an ice hockey rink, a swimming pool, a library, a school and a health centre. But the Inuit still hunt for meat instead of buying it from the shop. The old skills have not been forgotten completely.

Children at school in Igloolik. Their computer is programmed in the Inuit language. ▶

◄ *The Inuit can now buy food at convenience stores in Igloolik. But they prefer to hunt caribou, walrus, seal, fish or polar bear.*

Religion

Christian missionaries began to come to Igloolik before the Second World War. The new religions split the community in two. Sometimes the divisions were bitter. Leah Otak, an Anglican woman, remembered: 'When I was a girl, if I even looked at a Catholic boy I got into big trouble'.

Hunting

The sea near Igloolik is free of ice for eight or ten weeks each summer. The Inuit use this time to hunt, and the town almost empties. Whole families leave for hunting and fishing camps.

Back to the Old Ways

These children are asleep in an Outpost Camp. These are bases for people who have decided to go back to the old ways. They live off the land all year round.

▼ *Camping out on the ice sea.*

Many people would have to hunt for food even if they didn't enjoy it. There are very few jobs in Igloolik. People have to depend on money from the government. Hardly anyone could afford to eat nothing but expensive food shipped in by air from outside.

With the Sun peeping over the horizon behind him, a hunter waits above a hole in the ice. A seal that comes up to breathe will be harpooned. ▶

▲ *Snowmobiles parked outside an Inuit home.*

One problem in Igloolik is alcoholism. People drink too much alcohol and make themselves ill. Sometimes they even die. And often people who have drunk too much are unpleasant or violent towards others.

Despite this, Igloolik is a base for Inuit culture in the region. Many Inuit politicians have come from the village.

Alcohol and the Fur Trade

The fur traders started Inuit people drinking alcohol. They exchanged furs for bottles of cheap whiskey.

5 Hunting Today

An Inuit hunter from northern Greenland remembered: 'As I got closer to the whale, my heart was beating so loudly I thought the whale would hear it and dive'.

Hunting in the Arctic is exciting, but dangerous. Every year hunters are killed. They fall through the ice, or are swept out to sea on an ice floe, never to be seen again.

▲ *A hunter in Greenland harpoons a whale.*

◀ *A dog team helps to squeeze a walrus through a hole in the ice.*

In many ways, hunting has become easier than it was in the past. The Inuit have borrowed materials from outside and fitted them to the Inuit way of doing things. Sleds run more quickly with nylon runners, and motorboats are easier to fish from than kayaks. Hunting boots are lined with cotton wool instead of grass.

A hunter takes aim at a seal from behind a fabric screen. ▶

◄ *A hunter measures the tusks of a walrus he has killed. Inuit hunters help biologists to learn more about the animals of the Arctic by giving them this sort of information.*

In the old days, the Inuit's belief in the spirit world stopped them from overhunting. The spirits would have been angry and sent storms to trap the people in their homes, so they could not hunt any more.

Today, with the old beliefs gone and modern technology to help them, the Inuit could easily wipe out the animals they hunt. But they are careful never to kill too many. They do not want their children to starve because all the animals have been killed years ago. Some communities have stopped using motorboats and dog sleds, as a way of making sure that enough animals will be left.

▲ *In Thule, Greenland, Inuit hunt whales from kayaks using old-style harpoons. This makes sure they don't kill too many.*

▲ *Huntung walrus in northern Greenland.*

Pollution

The oil industry has brought terrible pollution to the Arctic's shores. In 1989, an oil tanker called the Exxon Valdez ran aground and spilt its cargo. The millions of gallons of oil in the sea will take years to clear up. In 1994, a pipeline in Siberia broke and spilt even more oil into the Arctic environment.

Other pollution is brought to the Arctic Sea by ocean and air currents from the south. If the region's pollution gets worse, it will soon be too dangerous to eat the meat of polar bears, seals and other animals. They will have taken in too many chemicals.

A seal. ▶
▼ *A polar bear.*

The Future for the Inuit

▲ *Inuit look out over the ice sea, at land they once had to themselves.*

In many ways, the future looks hard for the Inuit. The ways they think and act, whether they enjoy their lives or not, are all linked to hunting. If the Inuit cannot hunt, they will no longer be different to anyone else. They will no longer be Inuit.

Some of the changes that have come to the Inuit have been good. Their homes now have heat and light at the flick of a switch. They can move about more freely using motorboats, snowmobiles and, sometimes, helicopters and airplanes. The lives of the Inuit today are not so hard as they were a hundred years ago, and they live longer than in the past.

▲ *During the winter, helicopters are the only link with outside.*

◄ *An oil-drilling site in Alaska. The oil industry is one of the worst polluters of the Arctic environment.*

▲ *An Inuit village in Greenland. There, most people are Inuit, so they can make sure that things are done the Inuit way.*

Many of the changes that the Inuit have seen over the years have not been welcome. Outsiders encouraged the Inuit to trap animals for their furs. But now people think the fur trade is cruel, so the Inuit cannot sell the furs of the animals they hunt. Pollution of the Inuit hunting grounds is getting steadily worse, and could mean that hunting will have to stop entirely.

Nunavut

Nunavut means 'Our Land', the land the Inuit have always hunted on. Inuit groups in Canada have been trying since the 1970s to win back control of Nunavut.

▲ *Polar bears wander across the ice sea in the Canadian Arctic.*

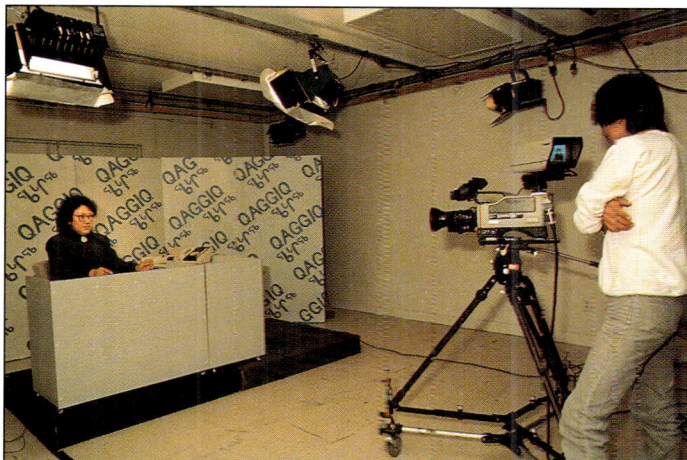

▲ *A snowmobile scoots across the ice, away from the setting sun.*

The Inuit think that they could run Nunavut better than it is being run at the moment.

After many years of struggle, the Inuit and the Canadian government signed an agreement in 1990. The Nunavut agreement will give the Inuit control of an area of land bigger than Norway.

Inuit TV

The Inuit want to make sure that their language does not die out. So they have started TV channels, newspapers and radio stations where all the words are in the Inuit language.

▲ An artist on Holman Island hangs a print up to dry.

The Nunavut agreement also provides the Inuit with money. The money is a payment for all the years the government used the Inuit's hunting grounds without asking them what they thought. Perhaps some of the money can be used to make things better for the Inuit.

Nunavut Money

Some of the money from Nunavut could be used to start Inuit businesses. For example, artists could buy materials and rent studios. Then they would be able to make money from their work.

Agreements like Nunavut cannot solve all the Inuit's problems. They cannot stop the pollution that drifts to the Arctic from elsewhere, for example. They cannot stop the demands of the oil and gas companies to be allowed to drill on Inuit land, although Nunavut will make it easier to resist them.

The Inuit had control of their land for centuries. They never polluted it, and they never wiped out any of the animals. Now, they want to win back control, so that they can try to prevent the situation getting worse.

▼ *These children may not be able to hunt as their ancestors and parents did. How will they live then?*

Glossary

Alaska A state of the USA that is separate from the rest. It lies far to the north, and stretches into the Arctic.

Angakkug A special person for the ancient Inuit, who helped them to contact the spirit world.

Anglican A member of one kind of Christian religion.

Arctic There are a lot of ways to describe the Arctic. One is the area within the Arctic Circle. Really the Arctic is the place far to the north where few plants grow and it is very cold.

Biologist A person who studies plants and animals.

Catholic A member of one kind of Christian religion.

Char A kind of tasty fish that is common in the Arctic.

Christian A member of a religion that believes that a man called Jesus Christ was the son of God.

Eskimo The name given to the Inuit by the Algonquin Indians who lived to the south. It means 'eater of raw meat'.

Homeland The place a people comes from.

Minerals Substances contained within rocks. Other things – metal or petrol, for example – can be made with minerals.

Missionaries Representatives of a religion who try to persuade others to follow their religion.

Further reading

Give Me My Father's Body Kenn Harper (Blacklead, 1986). The story of a young Inuit boy taken from his home by the explorer Robert Peary. This book is really for older readers, but is very interesting.

Inuit Bryan and Cherry Alexander (Wayland 1992). Explores the same ideas as this book, but in more detail.

What Do We Know About The Inuit? Bryan and Cherry Alexander (Macdonald Young Books, 1995).

Further information

Minority Rights Group
379 Brixton Rd
London SW9 7 DE

The Minority Rights Group produces learning material and information for teachers covering many aspects of minority rights.

Survival International
310 Edgeware Rd
London W2 1DY

Survival International is a worldwide movement to support tribal peoples. It stands for their rights to decide their own future and helps them protect their land and way of life.

There is a group for young people, called Young Survival. For a small membership fee you get a newsletter and the chance to buy games, T-shirts, tapes and other goods.

Index   Numbers in **bold** refer to pictures as well as text.